To Love Kindness

THE HEART OF COMPASSION

Bernard Häring, C.Ss.R.

LIGUORI CELEBRATION SERIES

Liguori

ONE LIGUORI DRIVE
LIGUORI MO 63057-9999

Imprimi Potest:
Richard Thibodeau, C.Ss.R.
Provincial, Denver Province
The Redemptorists

Imprimatur:
Most Reverend Michael J. Sheridan
Auxiliary Bishop, Archdiocese of St. Louis

ISBN 0-7648-0467-7
Library of Congress Catalog Card Number: 99-71464
© 1999, Munich Province of the Redemptorists
Printed in the United States of America
03 02 01 00 99   5 4 3 2 1

Scripture quotations from the *New Revised Standard Ver-
sion of the Bible,* © 1989 by the Division of Christian Education of the National Council of the Churches of Christ in the
USA. Used with permission. All rights reserved.

Quotations from Vatican II documents taken from *Vatican
Council II, the basic sixteen documents: Constitutions,
Decrees, Declarations. A completely revised translation in
inclusive language. Austin Flannery, OP, general editor.*
© *Costello Publishing Company: Northport, NY and
Dominican Publications: Dublin, Ireland (1996).*
This book is a revised edition of materials that originally
appeared in *Dare To Be Christian: Developing a Social Con-
science,* © 1983, Liguori Publications.

Cover design by Wendy Barnes

Table of Contents

Rejoice in God's Created Beauty

And in the spirit he carried me away to a great, high mountain and showed me the holy city Jerusalem coming down out of heaven from God. It has the glory of God and a radiance like a very rare jewel, like jasper, clear as crystal. It has a great, high wall with twelve gates....The wall is built of jasper, while the city is pure gold, clear as glass. The foundations of the wall of the city are adorned with every jewel; the first was jasper, the second sapphire, the third agate, the fourth emerald, the fifth onyx, the sixth carnelian, the seventh chrysolite, the eighth beryl, the ninth topaz, the tenth chrysoprase, the eleventh jacinth, the twelfth amethyst. And the twelve gates are twelve pearls, each of the gates is a single pearl, and the street of the city is pure gold, transparent as glass.

Revelation 21:10-12a,18-21

If the all-holy God draws us totally to the divine Self in order to make us a shining light for the world, God does so by the splendor of divine bounty, heavenly bliss, and the power of all the magnificent beauty God has revealed. To rejoice in beauty is an essential dimension of being human. If this is absent or inactive, there is no way we can approach the morality of the Beatitudes and the praise of God's glory.

Someone brought a beautiful bouquet of flowers to the sickbed of a man who was addicted to eating and drinking too much. He did not even look at them, but curtly asked the nurse to take them away, saying: "What good are these flowers? I can't eat or drink them!"

Obviously, there is nothing wrong with enjoying good food and wine, which are also God's gifts. These foreshadow the heavenly feast and remind us of the eucharistic meal. But can we imagine the joyous banquet with God and all the saints in heaven if our pleasure is restricted to what we will eat or drink? How wretched is the person who cannot rejoice in beauty, bounty, signs of friendship; who cannot admire and be grateful for what is good, true, and beautiful in itself! Nothing is left to such a one but hangovers and boredom.

Our sick man, who sees no meaning in beautiful flowers, was probably—in his healthy days—a great achiever and a hard worker, even boastful of his sense of duty. He is representative of a substantial part of our society which, despite its highly organized leisure-time activities, is appallingly empty: lacking aesthetic feeling, without appreciation for music, wanting in religious dimension, with no taste for the Good

News that both comes from and leads to God, and no appetite for an enthusiastic faith, or for gratitude and praise to God.

God did not create and redeem this world for mere consumption and production. Utility is not the prime motivation for men and women and the creation entrusted to them. The biblical account of creation evokes words of marvel and admiration; it elicits joy, thanksgiving, praise. To rejoice in something that is beautiful, without worrying whether it is useful, is a wonderful act of gratitude to God.

WHAT BEAUTY SAYS TO US

According to Saint Thomas Aquinas, beauty is one of the most characteristic names of God. Creation and redemption are revelations of God's glory and splendor of God's own beauty. The vision in the Book of Revelation, quoted at the beginning of this chapter, is an essential feature of God's promises. It presumes our taste for beauty.

Beauty speaks to us in our wholeness; it is attractive beyond all considerations of utility and profit. Loving people—beautiful and attractive themselves—discover the beauty, the goodness, the authenticity of others. They see others' inner resources and summon them to life. Openness to beauty unfolds in contemplation and is a most pleasant way to reach all that is good and true. Indeed, beauty itself is the splendor of what is true and good.

Those who have developed an appreciation for authentic beauty cannot be seduced by cheap sex appeal. They will seek out people who beautifully radiate truthfulness, kindness, serenity, peace. Such people are, of themselves, invitations to strive for good-ness and authenticity.

In its enchanting purity and integrity, beauty speaks to believers with an inner language that sings of the glory of a loving Creator; a God who, in every work, reveals the very beauty and generosity of the divine Self. Saint Augustine expresses a primary religious experience of millions of people when he prays:"How beautiful is everything which you have made! But how ineffably more beautiful are you, the Creator of all things!"

BEAUTY AND GLORY

The Holy Spirit is called not only the spirit of truth but also the "spirit of glory"(1 Peter 4:14).Those guided by the Spirit, in lives of constant gratitude and grateful service, are led to ever deeper and more blessed knowl-edge of the "Father of glory," the "Lord of glory and majesty."

"Glory" is a key word in Holy Scripture. Religious people speak of glory when they are wholly seized by God's attractive and awe-inspiring majesty, filled with joy by God's nearness and love, and by a fervent fear in the face of such holiness.

This basic experience of holy fear—of awe, marvel, and bliss—gives us strength to follow Christ crucified, in view of "the knowledge of the glory of God in the face of Jesus Christ" (2 Corinthians 4:6), for Jesus caused his light to shine within us.

When he is ready to drink the bitter chalice, and to accept the outrage of the cross, Jesus prays to his Father.

*The glory that you have given me I have given
them, so that they may be one, as we are one, I in
them and you in me, that they may become completely one, so that the world may know that you
have sent me and have loved them even as you
have loved me. Father, I desire that those also,
whom you have given me, may be with me where
I am, to see my glory, which you have given me
because you loved me before the foundation of
the world.*

John 17:22-24

Christians cannot think about everlasting happiness
without constantly praising God's glory and majesty;
without, as well, marveling at God's attractive and
awe-inspiring beauty—that beauty whose blissful and
resplendent rays already enlighten the faces of saints.

The biblical morality of the Beatitudes is a morality
of beauty and glory, infinitely more fruitful and attractive than a mere morality of duties and prohibitions.
When we develop the sense of beauty, we gain a better access and a more grateful relationship to the whole
of reality. Experiencing the boundless beauty of God's
good world, we open ourselves wholly to a morality
of grace and graciousness. We sense the depth of the
words of Saint Paul: "You are not under law but under
grace" (Romans 6:14).

THE GIFT OF BEAUTY

An inner relationship with beauty, in view of the
One who is Beauty, gives to Christian lives a note of
joy, courage, and creativity. Beauty is a gratuitous gift.
It does not cry out, "do this, do that," but transforms

the human mind and heart: intuition, spirit, and will. It forms personalities whose relationship with the realm of the good, the honest, the fitting, and the truth is inborn: Christians who find their joy in God.

This is shown in the lives of the saints. Think of Saint Francis of Assisi, and of his joy in whatever was beautiful, especially simple and ordinary things; or of Saint Alphonsus Liguori, so enraptured by the beauty of divine love and glory that in the midst of a sermon he could compose songs and sing the Good News into the hearts of the faithful.

Now, as always, the world needs saints who will educate people to appreciate beauty as it radiates the good and the true. This is an absolute necessity if we want to help our culture rise above its insensitive, sterile, producer/consumer mentality. Such a growth would do much for the liberation of our society from the ugliness of aggressiveness and violence.

Everyone is meant to become a masterpiece of God's love and, at the same time, co-artist in the wonderful work of forming others in God's authentic image. Each person can develop some dimension of art—of creativity. And, whatever our individual skills or limits in the human arts, we can all become experts in the *supreme art* of being loving and lovable people: of becoming saints and helping each other in this most glorious work of art. We have the divine promises. The world needs us to be beautiful, whole, and holy people.

Prayer

*God of glory and majesty, we praise you for all the
beauty of your creation: the bright firmament, the
green of our meadows, the quiet and healthy air
of the forests, the joy and splendor of flowers, the
love songs of birds, and the ever-new beauty of
myriad species of animals. Wherever we look, we
see the reflection of your own beauty inviting us to
marvel, to admire, to praise, and to thank you.*

*We praise you for each smile of a beloved child,
for the radiant faces of true lovers, for the
hope-inspiring beauty of mature graciousness in
so many people, for the magnificent wholeness of
holy people.*

*We praise you for your wonders in the history of
salvation, for the psalms and all the Holy Scriptures, which teach us to better discover the beauty
of all your works and the wisdom revealed in the
work of redemption.*

*Above all, we praise you for the great miracle of
the Incarnation of your beloved Son, Jesus Christ:
for his gracious kindness to all who came to him;
for the majesty of his forgiveness and love on the
cross; for the revelation of your glory in his
Resurrection; and for the promise of our resurrection in glory if our life here on earth glorifies your
majesty and love.*

*Lord, teach us to marvel, to admire, to praise, and
to thank you for your beauty and the beauty of all
your creation.*

Share Your Faith

Therefore take up the whole armor of God, so that you may be able to withstand on that evil day, and having done everything, to stand firm. Stand therefore, and fasten the belt of truth around your waist, and put on the breastplate of righteousness. As shoes for your feet put on whatever will make you ready to proclaim the gospel of peace. With all of these, take the shield of faith, with which you will be able to quench all the flaming arrows of the evil one. Take the helmet of salvation, and the sword of the Spirit, which is the word of God.

Ephesians 6:13-17

I regard everything as loss because of the surpassing value of knowing Christ Jesus my Lord. For his sake I have suffered the loss of all things, and I regard them as rubbish, in order that I may gain Christ and be found in him, not having a righteousness of my own that comes from the law, but one that comes through faith in Christ, the righteousness from God based on faith. I want to know Christ and the power of his resurrection and the sharing of his sufferings by becoming like him in his death, if somehow I may attain the resurrection from the dead.

Philippians 3:8-11

We find our identity, and discover the radiance of our witness and service, by means of faith. In faith, we recognize that everything comes from God, the Father of us all. Out of gratitude for the gift of faith and the joy that arises from faith, we dedicate ourselves to the service of the Gospel. When, in faith, we experience the power of God's grace, we know that what the world needs, above all else, is a share in this gift.

"God's armor" is not meant for mere self-defense; it symbolizes the faith with which Christians must face the world. This most precious gift allows us to "stand firm" while bringing "the gospel of peace" to human-kind. The "helmet of salvation" is linked with the "sword of the Spirit...the word of God." This is what the world needs most: God's people sharing the light, joy, and strength of faith, in gratitude for the gift of faith and joy which the Spirit gives. Saints are marked by the death of Christ and they live in conformity with it; but they are also people who experience "the power of his resurrection."

The "yes" of faith is essentially a grateful assent to the gift of faith that also indicates our readiness to follow in its path as a community of believers. In reference to our universal call to holiness, Vatican II speaks to all Christians: "All...according to their own gifts and duties must steadfastly advance along the way of a living faith, which arouses hope and works through love" (*Lumen Gentium*, "The Church," 41).

MEANING OF FAITH

Faith covers the whole of God's revelation. We believe in the living God who has revealed himself in Jesus Christ. Aristotle and other philosophers proved that there must be a prime cause setting all causes in movement. This is true, but it is far from what we believe if no mention is made that the prime cause is a God who is Love.

Deeply touched by the insight that Christian faith is infinitely more wonderful than the insights of the philosophers, Blaise Pascal wrote, with his own blood, his confession of faith in the God of history: [My God is] "not the god of the philosophers, but the God of Abraham, the God of Isaac, the God of Jacob, the God and Father of our Lord Jesus Christ." Our confession of faith proclaims praise of God arising from our innermost self. It is the life response to the One who is "God-with-us," who calls us to an intimate communion. In faith, we entrust ourselves to God, accept wholeheartedly our ineffable vocation, and dedicate ourselves to God's reign.

Faith which grants salvation is, for us, a great feast of love and trust. In the Old Testament, God revealed the divine Self as "spouse" of Israel. In Jesus Christ, the Godhead has espoused humanity forever in a permanent covenant between God and humankind. In Jesus Christ, God irrevocably enters into communion with us. God's love and mercy are without end. We are called to be the holy people of God, who has prepared for us an endless feast in which we share undying love with the Trinity.

In faith, each of us responds with our own unique name, but it must be remembered that God's life and revelation are to be shared by all people. Through our own faith experience—our mission and inner dynamic to share the joy of faith—we give witness to its joyful content as much as possible.

In faith, each of us rejoices in being loved by the One who is Love. But in faith, we rejoice as well in knowing that all are loved by God; all are invited to the love feast. In faith, we can individually marvel, wonder, adore. But what the world most needs today are believers who yearn for *all* people to come to the kind of joy and strength of faith that they have. It is natural that the author of Ephesians, in his eulogy on faith, invites believers to "pray in the Spirit at all times in every prayer and supplication [and] to that end [to] keep alert and always persevere in supplication for all the saints" (Ephesians 6:18).

DIMENSIONS OF FAITH

One dimension of Christian faith is the joyful celebration of the sacraments of faith in the festive community. Faith is shared in singing, in praising God in community, indeed, in all of life. Faith also gives us strength and motivation to bear each others' burdens.

I was deeply saddened once, when I heard a priest "boasting" that he never had any "faith experiences." He could not understand how people—even those who aren't priests—could have such experience. Poor man! There are Christians who have memorized the truths and duties of their faith; but what the world needs most is believers who have encountered faith experiences. It is a great privilege to live with Christians who are "on fire," filled with the joy and marvel of their faith. Where such communities exist, there is reliable witness to the Gospel, and recognition of being sent to share the joy and the Gospel of peace.

The Gospel was—is!—spread by Christians who are deeply touched by its truths; touched by the unlimited love of God revealed and made tangible in Jesus Christ, and revealed again and again in the lives of saints who direct all our attention to Christ and his Father.

Saints are not interested in the small pleasures of life, nor are they constantly concerned about their "self-fulfillment." They bear their own crosses, and are always willing to accept the burdens of others. Their secret was expressed long ago, by Esdras the priest: "The joy of the LORD is your strength" (Nehemiah 8:10c).

Mature Christians look on the moral implications of faith with the same kind of trust that they place in the divine promises. Deeply impressed, and changed by his encounter with Saint Francis of Assisi, a Roman cardinal capsulized the life and message of the saint: "We can, we will, we must live the Gospel." The "must" details the joy, the gratitude, the strength that arises by grace from the "can" and the "will." This is part of the inner dynamics of love. It is what makes the saints "witnesses"; what makes their lives a challenge for so many. The saints issue elegant invitations to the feast of faith, and to a firm commitment to the reign of God.

Faith establishes the conviction that we are invited to be friends of Jesus, children of God. There is no room for mediocrity. "For God did not call us to impurity but in holiness" (1 Thessalonians 4:7). Those who accept this vocation become blessings for their neighbors, for the call is clear: "Be perfect, therefore, as your heavenly Father is perfect" (Matthew 5:48).

COMMUNITY OF FAITH

Christians consider their personal vocations—to fullness of life, love, justice, and peace—as part of the

call of the whole Church to holiness. Christians know
that each individual fidelity concerns *all* the members
of the Mystical Body of Christ—indeed, of all humankind. "If one member suffers, all suffer together with
it; if one member is honored, all rejoice together with
it" (1 Corinthians 12:26).

Our faith is marked by our pilgrim condition. The
fundamental option implied in our faith response tends
gradually to permeate our whole being, making us ever
more conformed with Christ, more detached from
whatever might block our pilgrim path, and more free
to join in God's own liberating love of all people.

*As God's chosen ones, holy and beloved, clothe
yourselves with compassion, kindness, humility,
meekness, and patience. Bear with one another
and, if anyone has a complaint against another,
forgive each other; just as the Lord has forgiven
you, so you also must forgive. Above all, clothe
yourselves with love, which binds everything
together in perfect harmony.*

Colossians 3:12-14

When, by the strength of our faith, we put this into
practice, we help humanity to overcome its *spiritual*
"energy crisis," which is infinitely more serious than
the physical energy crisis.

Holy people live neither on an island nor in a ghetto.

*All Christians, in the conditions, duties, and cir-
cumstances of their lives and through all these,
will grow constantly in holiness if they receive all
things with faith from the hand of the heavenly
Father and cooperate with the divine will,*

*making manifest in their ordinary work the love
with which God has loved the world.*

Lumen Gentium, "The Church," 41

Prayer

*God, we praise you for the gift of faith which, in
so many holy people, has borne fruit in love for
the life of the world. We thank you for having
revealed, in Jesus Christ, your wonderful design
for all your people. We thank you for the community of faith, the Church, and for all believers who
radiate joy and peace and help us to understand
the real meaning of faith.*

*Thank you for parents and friends who have
enriched us through the strength and abundance
of their faith, and have treated us as sharers of the
eternal heritage. Thank you for the witness of
dying believers who give us glimpses of what faith
obtains, and of the kind of peace it radiates.*

*Lord Jesus, you have watched over your mission to
proclaim Good News to the poor, the downtrod-
den, the suffering. You have awakened in many
sick and depressed people a new hope, and you
can truly say to them, "Your faith has healed
you." Grant us a radiant faith; and give to the
world, which is so impoverished despite all its
material success, what it needs most: Christians
who dare to be joyful, faithful believers.*

Assist the Alienated

In your hearts sanctify Christ as Lord. Always be ready to make your defense to anyone who demands from you an accounting for the hope that is in you; yet do it with gentleness and reverence. Keep your conscience clear, so that, when you are maligned, those who abuse you for your good conduct in Christ may be put to shame.
1 Peter 3:15-16

Let us approach with a true heart in full assurance of faith, with our hearts sprinkled clean from an evil conscience and our bodies washed with pure water. Let us hold fast to the confession of our hope without wavering, for he who has promised is faithful. And let us consider how to provoke one another to love and good deeds, not neglecting to meet together, as is the habit of some, but encouraging one another, and all the more as you see the Day approaching.
Hebrews 10:22-25

While traveling by train one day, I met a fellow who struck up an intimate conversation with me. His only son, who was to inherit his father's business, had lost the faith. When the father gave him money, the son resented it and immediately passed it on to the poor, arguing that all the father's wealth was the result of an unjust economic system. Yet the son became angry when the father gave funds to pious or charitable works, saying that this, as well as the father's faith, was escapism—the unconscious hypocrisy of a rich man who treats his workers and employees as objects.

We had a long talk, and the man made a soul-searching examination of conscience. His son's loss of faith was of much greater concern to the father than the future of his business. He was willing to change his conduct radically in the economic and political spheres, with the intent of finally giving his son and others a convincing witness of faith.

I had a similar experience when I lectured in the Philippines on the social implications of the Sermon on the Mount. A very wealthy lady, owner of large sugar plantations, was extremely affected by my words. She realized that her conduct, and that of other land owners, was causing a deep crisis of faith among the workers, who lived in misery and were totally dependent upon their employers. She came to me for advice and help. She was willing to make the most radical changes, giving all who worked for her a just share of the profits and allowing them to participate in decision-making procedures. But she felt threatened by the powerful land owners, who would treat her as a traitor if she would dare to act according to her conscience.

SIGNS OF ALIENATION

One of the most alarming and challenging signs of our times is that almost all of us have alienated relatives, friends, or neighbors, and we cannot avoid the hard questions about our own accountability for these broken relationships.

The numbers of unchurched people are rapidly growing in many countries of the Western world. Our culture is marked to a considerable extent by a tendency toward unbelief; there is little room left for God in our society and its economy. A large part of the world is dominated by bureaucracies that use their power—from systematic training to secret police, from legislation to methodical manipulation of minds through the mass media—to inculcate their own brands of atheism into a subjugated people.

Vatican II, with sincere soul-searching, dealt with the problem of today's atheism (see *Gaudium et Spes,* "The Church in the Modern World," 19-22). We would do well to meditate on this text as background for our own personal examinations of conscience.

Church leaders asked themselves—and each one of us—to what extent we are all accountable for the increasing unbelief in the world. The shocking phenomenon of atheism in our own neighborhoods urges us even to ask ourselves about the "hidden atheist" in our individual hearts and minds, actions and inactions. We should, however, avoid extremism in our search for answers. We should not impute to ourselves and Church institutions such guilt as would seem to leave the atheist guiltless.

OUR RESPONSE

There are certain wholesome responses we can make. We can renew our interest in the community of faith, thus strengthening and deepening our own faith and the faith of our believing brothers and sisters. Then, in a shared effort, we can more easily rid ourselves of any contamination of atheism, driving it out from the hiding places it has found in our hearts and in our lifestyles. Our main concern, in view of the mission of the Church and the needs of the world, should be to give a convincing witness of our faith and final hope.

The Council's reflections on and examinations of the various forms and shades of atheism should open our eyes to the severity of this problem. Its words are a clarion call to a more radical conversion to faith and all its implications in life.

Today's achiever/consumer society offers an educational system mainly geared to attain success as bureaucrats, business and professional people, and scientists—giving little attention to the formation of mature personalities, with depth and breadth of vision and firmness of character.

The educational system, and the whole success-oriented lifestyle, entice both youths and adults to cultivate knowledge for domination, utility, success, and career—and this is done so intensely and exclusively that there is little time to acquire knowledge of wholeness and salvation. Even the behavioral sciences, which customarily make valuable contributions to human growth, frequently deprive themselves of their beneficial dynamics by concentrating on a small sector of research. Thus the spirit of wholeness is lost.

If we are truly concerned about our alienated brothers and sisters, and especially our youth, then we shall do all we can to change our educational systems and our lifestyles. If we ourselves, by the grace of God, possess a sense for the mystical and a vision of wholeness, we will support all efforts to make this sense and this vision possible in our culture. If we all strive for wholeness and holiness ourselves, we can have confidence that God will grant, in our time, many saints who are outstanding in these valuable qualities.

Ernst Bloch, the Marxist philosopher, embodies in his writings the atheist who cannot and will not believe in a God above us because such an unbeliever refuses to be anybody's debtor. Atheists think it undermines our dignity to thank a God for having granted us unmerited gifts. In view of this, could not our lives and behavior as believers make it more evident that it is this very gratitude—the recognition that everything is gift—that awakens our creativity and fosters respect and care for others?

There are unbelievers who want to eliminate the "God question," or at least subordinate it, in order to honor humankind more effectively as the be-all and end-all of creation. Again, a question: Should not believers show more convincingly that faith reveals the full dignity of every human being, and that nothing can move others to respect the dignity and liberty of all people more than our lived faith in a God who has created everyone in the divine image and likeness?

The Council alerts us to the fact that there are "unbelievers" who, in reality, do not deny the true God but are protesting against a people-made, false image of God. Could we not, through our own hunger and thirst for a better knowledge of the *true* God and our adoration "in spirit and truth," help these people to discover explicitly their own yearning for the true God? This demands, above all, that we see in Jesus Christ the true image of God—that we resist all temptations to make ourselves self-styled "images of God."

The most dangerous—and perhaps the most common—form of "godlessness" is an absolute lack of interest in the "God question" coupled with the same lack of interest in the ultimate meaning of life. Some of today's godless people are not even interested enough to *deny* God's existence, or to think or speak about the subject. Their concerns are totally oriented to success, power, pleasure, and similar objectives.

This form of godlessness is the strongest challenge for Christians. We cannot alleviate this alienation if the same fleeting and disruptive interests occupy pride of place in our own lifestyles, even if we are also—but in second place—seeking to know, love, and serve God. This widespread attitude is, in itself, an expression of polytheism: We place other gods on a par with the true God when we do not reserve for God the first place—indeed, the *whole* place—in our hearts.

The Bible texts at the beginning of this chapter show us that words alone are not convincing and liberating responses to the problems, wounds, and needs of the alienated. Intelligent and competent use of dialogue are important factors, but prime consideration must be given to total witness by our lives. Then our words and gestures will arise from a joyous, grateful faith, and a profound trust in the divine promises.

Faith and life must be harmonized, but never in the direction of the lowest common denominator. If there

is a distressing distance between the loftiness of our
faith and the quasi-mediocrity of our lives, our alienated sisters and brothers should be able to at least sense
how much this pains us and how sincerely we are striving to bridge the gap.

FAMILY CRISES

These reflections on the alienated should be distin-
guished from the painful experiences of good Christian parents when their children go through crises of
faith and, in some cases, even say they have lost their
faith. These are very complex affairs, which differ from
case to case, but which are often intensified by atheis-
tic or secularist surroundings in school and aggravated
by the mass media and the general environment.

Here is an example of just such a crisis. A mother
and father asked me to accept an appointment with
their daughter, a young lady who had told her parents
that she could no longer receive the sacraments
because she had lost her faith. She came willingly, and
spoke with true sincerity. At one point in our dialogue,
I asked if her search for God was her greatest concern.
She answered with a simple "Yes," but later qualified it:
"Maybe my greatest concern is the fear that I shall not
be able to give my own children, in the future, the
joyous faith that has marked my parents' life."

I reassured her: "As I see it, you are by no means an
unbeliever. As long as this search takes first place in
your heart and mind—despite your present crisis of
faith—God will accept it. Perhaps you are now closer
to God than you were in your uncritical phase."
Indeed, she was on the road to a more mature faith.
Can all of us who call ourselves believers so sincerely

say that the concern to know God and follow God's will takes first place in our lives?

Another experience touched my heart deeply. A family had four boys, one of whom was born blind. All members of the family were always cheerful with the blind boy, but never dared to talk directly about his blindness. For a considerable time, everything went well. The boy received First Communion with great fervor, and for two years he received the sacrament each Sunday with his family. Then, one Sunday, he did not join them when they went to Communion. The parents thought it best not to question him. Later that week, when it was his turn to say the blessing at table, the boy said firmly: "I don't pray anymore; I cannot believe that God is good."

For some years, this situation continued. Finally, one day he began to speak with his parents about his blindness and all its consequences. He explicitly stated his doubt about God's goodness and justice, but his words now sounded like his search was coming to an end. The family began to feel that he was gradually accepting his disability.

One Sunday, he again went with his parents to Communion, and gave them an immediate explanation: "I can believe and pray again." Not much later, he said: "I think I am finally mature enough to receive confirmation. I know now what it means to be a Christian."

In both of these cases, the children were blessed with parents who gave them trusting support as well as abiding love and respect. Their parents allowed these children to find their own ways through the crisis. In both cases too, there was a clear growth of faith in the whole family.

The alienated, whether in our own family or in the world that surrounds us, need all the help that we can give them.

Prayer

Gracious God, thank you for the gift of faith. It is due to your grace and patience that, despite the gaps between faith and life, we remain faithful. Thanks to you, we have dialogued with many other believers who have helped our faith to grow and become more deeply rooted. Praised be your graciousness forever!

Help us to better understand our unbelieving and alienated brothers and sisters. Guide us in our dealings with them, so that we might say the right words at the right time, and show us how to accept their challenge by making a firmer decision to live according to our faith, deepening it in all its dimensions.

Holy God, send forth your Spirit. Fill us with the desire to find ways to heal our culture, which becomes for so many a cause of unbelief. Inspire us to form a more lively community of believers, and to seek light and strength from the celebration of the sacraments of faith. Help us to take more seriously our mission to be "the light of the world."

Father of us all, come to the aid of parents who are at a loss when facing the unhappy crises of faith in their children. Guide our young people in their dark days, so that they may find their way to a mature and firm faith.

Be Faithful

The saying is sure: If we have died with him, we will also live with him; if we endure, we will also reign with him; if we deny him, he will also deny us; if we are faithless, he remains faithful—for he cannot deny himself.
2 Timothy 2:11-13

I give thanks to my God always for you because of the grace of God that has been given you in Christ Jesus, for in every way you have been enriched in him, in speech and knowledge of every kind—just as the testimony of Christ has been strengthened among you—so that you are not lacking in any spiritual gift as you wait for the revealing of our Lord Jesus Christ. He will also strengthen you to the end, so that you may be blameless on the day of our Lord Jesus Christ. God is faithful; by him you were called into the fellowship of his Son, Jesus Christ our Lord.
1 Corinthians 1:4-9

One of the most alarming signs of our times is the shocking lack of faithfulness. Such a lack of faithfulness is a sign of lack of faith. Married Christians, for example, commit adultery and obtain civil divorces in nearly the same proportions as do unbelievers. Where there is unselfish faithfulness and generous forgiveness, there is the presence of faith. The world needs both the joyous faith and the unbroken faithfulness of these who are in a genuine pursuit of holiness.

Holy Scripture sings in sundry melodies the praise of God's faithfulness; but when it praises human fidelity it does so only in view of God's own faithfulness to covenant and promise. We praise God, above all, for that saving justice and mercy by which God restores faithless sinners to renewed constancy. Even God praises those faithful servants and stewards in whom are found mirror images of God's own faithfulness—a faithfulness that invites each of us to this stalwart virtue.

Our fundamental option of faith is at the same time a vow of fidelity. In faith, when we entrust ourselves totally to God, we offer praise through our constancy. The more firmly we walk on the path of faithfulness, the more our faith comes to its full development.

In the sacraments of faith, believers consciously meet God's favor and faithfulness. In fruitful celebration, we affirm our grateful acceptance of our vocation in allegiance to the covenant by which God binds us to God's self and calls us to mutual fidelity. The whole of our lives should echo the "Amen" of the liturgy, wherein we solemnly proclaim our "Yes" to a faithful God who calls us to abiding fidelity.

GOD'S FAITHFULNESS

*As surely as God is faithful, our word to you has
not been "Yes and No." For the Son of God, Jesus
Christ, whom we proclaimed among you...was
not "Yes and No"; but in him it is always "Yes."
For in him every one of God's promises is a "Yes."
For this reason it is through him that we say the
"Amen," to the glory of God. But it is God who
establishes us with you in Christ and has anointed
us, by putting his seal on us and giving us his
Spirit in our hearts as a first installment.*

2 Corinthians 1:18-22

Whenever we say "Amen" in our prayers, it should
be a conscious, trustful confirmation of our fundamental option for faith and fidelity, to the praise of God's
own faithfulness.

Jesus is the supreme sign and sacrament of God's
faithfulness in his covenant with humanity. In Jesus
Christ, and by the power of the Spirit, we are restored
in the covenant and called to a renewed and growing
fidelity. Christ is the abiding sign of both God's effica-
cious grace and humanity's response. Having come
from the Father, he has given, once and for all, his faithful response to the Father in the name of a redeemed
humankind.

Jesus verifies his faithfulness to God's design and
covenant in his total readiness for solidarity with sinful humanity. He, who has taken upon himself the burden of our sins and our misery, gives us the gifts of the
Spirit so that we can bear each other's burdens. Jesus'

faithfulness makes his disciples one with each other
and light for the world (see John 17:11-21).

OUR PERSONAL FIDELITY

If we hope to conform ourselves to Christ's faithfulness, to become effective signs of his call to fidelity,
we first must rid ourselves of wrong ideas about the
true meaning of faithfulness. Many people seem to
confuse fidelity with habit, with mere passivity, clinging to human traditions which either have lost their
original meaning or have never been actual signs of
faithfulness to God's holy presence.

Lessons from the prophets and saints encourage us
to live the Gospel and faithfully proclaim it ever anew.
Conscious of God's nearness, we do this even when it
means leaving the beaten paths on which many still
tread.

Faithfulness that arises from a living faith has nothing to do with blind submissiveness or apathetic
observance of external laws. Christians who are guided
by the Spirit know the ultimate law of faithful love
and the deepest meaning of all authentic laws. Any
loyalties to causes or groups will always be measured
by fidelity to Christ. Faithfully following in his foot-
steps, we can expose any undeserved loyalties

"Yes" to God's call to faithfulness implies the courage to take risks when necessary, to set out on new
paths in the history of salvation—like Abraham, the
prophets, the saints, and especially Jesus. Faithfulness
to the Gospel guarantees Christian identity by calling
us to a continuing process of conversion and growth,
to an ever more creative and generous fidelity.

Our faithfulness to the Church entails much more

than mere observance of laws. The Church needs Christians who make creative use of their talents and charisms for its mission and inner growth. Faithful servants do not bury their talents in the earth so that they can be given back without risk (see Matthew 25:24-30). What Christian faithfulness means is best expressed by the biblical passage about the gifts and fruits of the Spirit. Fidelity to the Spirit denotes creativity for the life of the world.

When we are guided by the Spirit, we know that true faithfulness to our own identity and vocation is possible only in faithfulness to God and in solidarity with the children of God. We find our true self in loving service to God and to all humanity.

Fidelity to self must be realistic. Even the most devout sometimes encounter doubt within themselves. We always need further conversion, so as to grasp our faith more fully and faithfully renew our fundamental option to faithfulness. The more we praise God for the steadfast faithfulness manifested to us, the more truthful will be our own professions of belief.

OUR FIDELITY TO OTHERS

In our response to God's fidelity, we more easily discover the grace-filled possibilities of fidelity to others. Faithfulness to God is the solid foundation of all human constancy and this, in turn, is an essential expression of our response to God's fidelity to us. But our "Amen" to God has its limits. It is authentic only if we journey together toward an ever more thorough fidelity to God.

The covenant of fidelity between two persons in marriage constitutes a risk because both partners are sources of risk. In a similar way, the same is true of religious vows, in that consecration to God's kingdom implies a covenant between a community and an individual. Yet, we dare this risk without anguish when our mutual *"yeses"* are given and integrated into the covenant with God, the source of all human fidelity. Time and again, we are forced to submit ourselves humbly to God's healing and forgiving faithfulness. There, we also learn that mutual reconciliation and forgiveness are essential parts of covenant fidelity.

Even should the marriage covenant be broken by one, to the point where healing is impossible, the abandoned spouse needs to strive faithfully to express forgiving love. A refusal to forgive can destroy the integrity and health of the "innocent" one. Indeed, in the eyes of God, nobody is innocent who does not forgive in conformity with God's merciful and healing fidelity.

God admonishes us, in many ways, to be faithful unto death. The divine warnings given to the unfaithful servant are to be understood in the context of the promise that God wills to perfect the work that has been begun. Nothing will be lacking for us if we turn to God in humble and faithful prayer. It is unmistakably the doctrine of the Church that the grace of perseverance unto death is an undeserved gift; but it is equally unmistakable that God wants to give this grace to all the redeemed. We pray sincerely for this gift, while constantly striving to honor God's saving faithfulness by forgiving and healing faithfulness toward our sisters and brothers. A legitimate interest in our own salvation implies total dedication to God's reign of love, justice, and peace. We do not forget that salvation and holiness imply solidarity; but it is foolish to imagine that we can possibly help in the salvation, well-being, and faithfulness of the world while neglecting our own salvation and faithfulness to God's gracious love.

Prayer

We praise you, loving God! Faithful to your name, and with boundless mercy, you have not abandoned sinful humankind in its self-caused misery. In your faithfulness, you have gone so far as to send us your own Son as the faithful sign and witness of your holiness, love, and mercy.

We praise your glory, for in the history of creation and salvation you have chosen us to be not only recipients but also coworkers and witnesses of your faithfulness and mercy, and have not stripped us of this wonderful dignity in spite of our failures.

We thank you, Lord Jesus Christ, that in the work of redemption you have sealed—by your death on the cross—your Father's and your own faithfulness with the blood of the covenant. We thank you for having offered to your Father, in the name of all of us whom you came to redeem, your priceless tribute of faithfulness; and we bless you for having called us to join you in praise of your loving Father by a life renewed in fidelity.

Lord Jesus, send us the Holy Spirit to teach us how to be open to your kingdom and to be faithful servants and witnesses for the life of the world which is so much in need of fidelity.

Listen To and Care For the Aged

If you gathered nothing in your youth, how can you find anything in your old age? How attractive is sound judgment in the gray-haired, and for the aged to possess good counsel! How attractive is wisdom in the aged, and understanding and counsel in the venerable! Rich experience is the crown of the aged, and their boast is the fear of the Lord.

Sirach 25:3-6

The way we relate to the aged and their social relevance reveals our fidelity to the past or our lack of it. In the Western world, the social problems of the aged are acute; in many aspects, they are a symptom of a sick society.

There has always been some kind of generation gap. In the Scriptures, we find many words of wisdom about attitudes toward the old. There evidently was a need to urge younger generations to honor the aged and to learn from their knowledge. But there is ample evidence also that, generally, the culture of the biblical era showed great reverence and a sense of gratitude toward the aged.

MANY PROBLEMS

In our times, the "generation gap" has become an acute problem. In a time of rapid cultural change, dialogue between the generations takes on tremendous importance, but it also becomes much more difficult. The cultural diversity between the younger and older generations raises barriers to mutual understanding and enrichment. The horizon of understanding has changed profoundly, and so has the distance between old and young. Households no longer provide the opportunity for intergenerational living. Not infrequently, the elderly have the feeling of being ignored. This feeling is particularly strong in nursing homes which are run according to economic considerations alone. In most industrialized and urban countries, the suicide rate among the elderly is very high. Often, it is preceded by the painful feeling of a kind of "social" death, the sad experience of being considered "useless." Media, the medical professions, even governments debate the "right" of the old and sick to euthanasia. The elderly who feel pushed aside understand this talk as an indirect invitation to disappear from the theater of life. This, of course, is not just a problem for the aged; it is a shocking indication of a sick society.

Some years ago, this was a serious social problem in rural areas when the old did not hand over their farms or business operations to the younger generation at the customary time. Today, people retire from their professional activities at age sixty or sixty-five, often when they are still vigorous and not at all ready to become inactive. Many are unprepared for the sudden change, and do not know how to profit by their leisure time or how to find an activity that interests them. This is especially true of those who have no meaningful social and cultural contacts, no real friendships.

Add to this the high inflation rate in many countries that robs people of their savings. Even where a high standard of social security prevails, bureaucratic bungling often causes distress. Single women are still widely discriminated against. Women's household work and the education they provide for their children are not considered socially important tasks, and even for paid jobs they do not receive salaries or pensions commensurate with that of men.

While in earlier times senior citizens could be proud of their role and their dignity as elders, the modern cult of youthfulness deprives them of this satisfaction. All this aggravates the task of aging: of accepting the many ailments, the gradual loss of hearing, the diminution of sight and strength.

SOME SOLUTIONS

Much has been done and is being done in many countries to ease the end of life's journey for the elderly. However, the longer life span and the consequent increased proportion of elderly citizens forces all of us—Church, state, families, trade unions, individuals—to think seriously about the best way to approach the social problems of the aged.

In the Church of the first centuries, the aged were community leaders or advisors. The term for priests, "elders" *(presbyteri)*, arose from this situation, which indicates that the elders were active in the apostolate. In some countries today, the Church garners many vocations for the permanent diaconate, and even for the priesthood and religious life, from the ranks of the "retired" who are still vigorous and willing to use their energies and life's wisdom for the service of God's reign in this pilgrim Church.

Many senior citizens exhibit great interest in continuing education. Church and society should make this and other appropriate privileges and outlets available for them, so that their knowledge and life experience may be fruitful for them and for others.

One of the saddest parts of aging is loneliness. We treasure the fact that to visit the sick and the lonely is an important work of mercy, but this must not become a "condescending" mercy which might offend the lonely. We want them to feel that we enjoy listening to them and learning from them. Children and grandchildren should feel especially privileged to make friendly visits to parents and grandparents.

Those who feel lonely, but are still spiritually and physically strong, could best overcome their loneliness by visiting other ailing and lonely people, by offering them some services, reading to them, helping them to pray. It is in this context we understand better the well-known text: "Are any among you sick? They should call for the elders of the church and have them pray over them, anointing them with oil in the name of the Lord" (James 5:14).

"Houses of prayer" have contributed valuable inspirational leadership in this area. All the members of these prayer houses participate in spontaneous shared prayer and faith dialogue, but it is especially the older members who dedicate themselves most vigorously to the lonely and sick, bringing them consolation and deeper understanding of their situation.

Many religious, after successful careers in teaching, have found this apostolate the highlight of their lives. They bring Communion to the lonely and the homebound. Greatly consoled by such visits from religious and other lay people, some have written to their bishops asking whether these visitors may be allowed to administer the sacrament of anointing of the sick because: "Father is always in a hurry, rushing in for the anointing and rushing out; but Sister takes time to listen to us and help us grasp the meaning of sickness and suffering." Unfortunately, at the present time the Church does not allow this special ministry to people not ordained to the priesthood. Meanwhile, however, senior citizens should continue to visit the lonely and console them with their faith presence and their prayers. And, in a way, that has much to do with the "anointing" of which the Letter of James speaks.

Much more could be done in this area, but for the present this spiritual and pastoral care for the lonely must serve as a steppingstone for further shared efforts in our struggle to solve the social problems of the elderly in our culture.

Prayer

Lord our God, we thank you for the gift of our older brothers and sisters: for their wisdom, their kindness, and their willingness to share life experiences with us. We thank you especially for those older men and women who radiate holiness and joy. Grant that we—both adults and youths— may gladly follow the guidance you give through the Scriptures in our care for the aged.

Assist the old and the lonely who are hurt by neglect and social alienation. Help them to resolve their problems and find meaning for their sufferings in the spirit of faith. Enlighten them on how to make creative use of their remaining years, and let them know that their growth in these days will benefit both them and others.

Lord, inspire the influential men and women in state and society to resolve the sometimes shocking problems of the aged, and to correct the many injustices under which they suffer today.

Guide your Church, so that, following the example of the early Christians, we may be vigilant, wise, and courageous in giving the elderly every opportunity to make use of their generous abilities in pursuit of their own special apostolate.

Give Youth
a Chance

I am writing to you, fathers, because you know him who is from the beginning. I am writing to you, young people, because you have conquered the evil one. I write to you, children, because you know the Father. I write to you, fathers, because you know him who is from the beginning. I write to you, young people, because you are strong and the word of God abides in you, and you have overcome the evil one.
1 John 2:13-14

Do not speak harshly to an older man, but speak to him as to a father, to younger men as brothers, to older women as mothers, to younger women as sisters—with absolute purity.
1 Timothy 5:1-2

If elders are an inducement to gratitude and faithfulness to the past, the young are a challenge to hope and a commitment to the future. Of course, all our relationships must be marked by grateful appreciation of the remembered past, but we must at the same time be alert to the present and confident of the future.

Our confidence, which looks to the promises of salvation history, and our responsibility for our own future and that of all humankind, will determine our attitudes toward youth. The future of both Church and society hinges on our investment in caring for youth, in educating our children and adolescents for co-responsibility. An open-minded dialogue with youth will keep us spiritually young.

From this perspective, we can see more clearly the obligations posed by responsible parenthood: the conscientious decision to bring children into the world and to educate them properly. This is the most valuable investment for humanity's future if the transmissions of life and lifestyle are accompanied by the cultivation of faith, hope, and love.

Many married couples refuse to transmit life because they have no gratitude for the past, no trust in the future, and no appreciation of the worth of the present moment. Others are simply discouraged by the difficulty of educating children properly in our muddled society. But couples who are blessed by mutual love, filled with gratitude for the gift of life and the hope of life everlasting, and able to make the most creative use of present opportunities will always have the courage to say "yes" to their parental vocation.

Responsible parenthood in an earlier, more static society achieved an education totally geared to the formation of responsible men and women. In a uniform, harmonious culture, a common faithfulness to inherited traditions and customs served to integrate the children into that culture and its values. Given those conditions, the respect about which Paul writes to Timothy, cited at the beginning of this chapter, was quite possible: parents treating their children like brothers and sisters in Christ, as coheirs of eternal life. In that closed society, a "good education" meant also a genuine internalization of faith, hope, and love, and of everything that is good, true, and beautiful.

For Christian parents, the goals of education are essentially the same today; but the uniqueness of our present situation necessitates a different emphasis and some additional perspectives.

This new look is a result of rapid cultural change, pluralism of world views and lifestyles, and the tremendous influence of the mass media. TV has become the new foster parents for many children. Mere adaptation to present circumstances—especially if this is coupled with a demand for blind obedience—would simply be a catastrophe. When only passivity and submissiveness are taught in childhood, this often leads to rebellion during adolescence and/or to submissiveness to the dominant forces of the environment in which the young adult will live.

PROMOTING RESPONSIBILITY

The main emphasis in education, therefore, must be on becoming responsible and discerning persons. The old values are not to be abandoned, but they should be qualified and integrated into a vision of wholeness, holiness, responsibility, and discernment.

Away from their Christian environment, our young people hear much talk about freedom, protest, and the search for self-fulfillment; but they hear little about faithfulness to God, love of neighbor, and self-examination of personal values. It is especially important, therefore, that Christian education should explain and cultivate, by witness and word, freedom in Christ, respect for the freedom and conscience of others, establishment of healthy relationships with God and humankind, creative faithfulness, and discernment which involves healthy self-examination.

Parents and other family members, teachers, and pastors must be aware that it is normal for youth to go through certain crises—for instance, through a phase of protest and doubt. If they do not profit from this phase, there is little hope that adolescents and young adults will be able to withstand the many dangers of being manipulated by false ideologies, or by the mass media which pressures them to accept prevailing immoral fads.

We must continue to learn and relearn how to dialogue with young people, for their reactions change considerably from one year to the next. We have also to free ourselves from stereotypical ideas about youth. There is great diversity among the young, and within every group each adolescent has the right to be seen in his or her own uniqueness.

As young people approach adulthood, a certain maturity is demanded of them. They must be prepared to make important decisions about their lives. Foremost among these are a firm determination to be faithful to God and God's reign, and a conscientious effort to choose their life's vocation wisely. Young people should be able to learn from us that their true identity rests on the strength of their faithfulness. When we show firmness and consistency in making our own decisions, children will see that the important decisions of life are built on faithfulness to conscience, even in minor matters.

Young Christians should also come to understand that all of life's decisions that are faithful to one's fundamental option are enlightened, strengthened, and enriched by the sacraments. Their baptismal vow is reinforced by their vow of confirmation, uplifting and sustaining them with the gifts and fruits of the Holy Spirit (see Galatians 5:22). These are the weapons for fighting against humanity's innate selfishness— whether collective or individual or both.

SHARING RESPONSIBILITY

Participation in church or civic groups and societies should help the young to develop and to exercise their creative energies. Adolescents and young adults should be treated as partners and given the chance to exercise co-responsibility with adults.

Because of the extended number of subjects provided by our educational systems, there is some danger that young people may absorb the subject matter only passively. All those responsible for education in family, school, society, and state should offer young people sufficient challenge and abundant opportunity for cooperation in creative liberty and fidelity.

This also holds for the political field. A party whose "old guard" insists on clinging to outmoded traditions simply penalizes itself and jeopardizes its future. The experience and wisdom of those who have grown up in dignity and have competently taken their share of responsibility is to be admired; but those who think themselves irreplaceable are lacking in wisdom.When young people have the ability, and are willing to acquire competence and able to share in responsibility, they should be given the chance to exercise these functions. In all sectors of public life, in society and Church, we need the spirit, courage, and imagination of youth.

Throughout the world, the unemployment of youth is a most serious and frightening problem. Not without reason has Pope John Paul II insisted that if this problem is to be dealt with effectively, it must be given high priority. Long-lasting unemployment is not only a grave danger for the psychic and social life of youth, but also a great loss for society. It should be evident to all responsible persons that it is easier to create jobs for youth than to rescue them from drug addiction, alcoholism, and violence.

A distinctively Christian vision of hope and solidarity gives us strong motivation to help children and youth to discover and to cultivate the contemplative dimension of life, to find in prayer how to bring genuine harmony into their lives. A good number of today's youth have shown themselves open to faith dialogues, to shared prayer, to joy in the praise of God; however, they should be careful to avoid formalism.They are in search of authentic religious experience. They need holy people to help them along the way.

Prayer

*God, our Father, Lord of history, you love children
and young people. You rejoice in their growth
toward maturity. Give to all of us the openness
and joy in creative activities exhibited by the
young. Look with favor upon our youth, for whom
today's culture can be a great challenge but also,
alas, a great danger.*

*Give our young people courage to be faithful, to
accept their share of responsibility, to search
diligently for life's ultimate meaning and purpose,
to place their trust in you, and to show a reason-
able trust in the future of humanity which
depends so much on their active participation in
shaping it.*

*Grant us the ability and the desire to accept
youth, to love them as they are, and to appreciate
them as persons who can offer dimensions which
we are no longer able to offer. Help us to accept
them fully as fellow pilgrims and partners on the
road to eternal life, and to aid them in their
efforts to shape history to the benefit of coming
generations. Inspire us with confidence in our
young people, for we can learn much from them.*

*Lord, grant to your Church the prophetic vision
needed to rid itself of outmoded customs. May we
gladly proclaim the Gospel to youth, while living it
boldly in today's world. And may we continue to
welcome the willing generosity of young people in
their efforts to become active workers in God's
reign.*

Glorify God in Your Body

Jesus answered them, "Destroy this temple, and in three days I will raise it up." The Jews then said, "This temple has been under construction for forty-six years, and will you raise it up in three days?" But he was speaking of the temple of his body. After he was raised from the dead, his disciples remembered that he had said this; and they believed the scripture and the word that Jesus had spoken.

John 2:19-22

[We are] always carrying in the body the death of Jesus, so that the life of Jesus may also be made visible in our bodies. For while we live, we are always being given up to death for Jesus' sake, so that the life of Jesus may be made visible in our mortal flesh. So death is at work in us, but life in you. But just as we have the same spirit of faith that is in accordance with scripture— "I believed, and so I spoke"—we also believe, and so we speak, because we know that the one who raised the Lord Jesus will raise us also with Jesus, and will bring us with you into his presence.

2 Corinthians 4:10-14

The whole human person should be and continue to become an ever more attractive image of God. A human countenance that radiates joy, peace, kindness, gentleness, cordiality, and compassion is sure to awaken in others a great longing to see God's glorious countenance in Jesus Christ. The mere sight of hands clasped in friendship, guaranteeing trust and understanding, makes it easier for many to pray to God, "Into thy hands I commend my spirit." We stretch out our hands as a sign of cordial greeting or of reconciliation, and accept gratefully the other's hand as a sign of harmony and fidelity.

In basic ways, the human body expresses the spirit that lies within. Even at a distance, do we not know from the lift of the head and the speed of the feet that this is a messenger who is bringing good news? Conversely, when we see the step of those trained in military maneuvers, do we not also hear in the distance the noise of war and the cry of the oppressed?

Holy Scripture gives us a magnificent vision of the human body. Jesus praises his Father: "A body you have prepared for me....I have come to do your will, O God" (Hebrews 10:5b,7b). His hands dispense blessing, touch the blind, the deaf, the sick, and the sinners with healing love and power. His gracious countenance consoles the afflicted. And, finally, on the cross he stretches out his arms in all-embracing love for the whole of humanity. His voice not only echoes the cry of the suffering poor, but also speaks words of concern, forgiveness, love, consolation, and promise. His pierced heart becomes the fountain of salvation.

Jesus calls his body a "temple" in which God is glorified and which, raised to life again by the Father, will be glorious for all eternity. All temples built by human hands take second place to the bodies of the children of God, conformed to the body of the beloved Son, Jesus Christ. Christ has given the greatest sign of love by giving up his body on the cross for his brothers and sisters (see 1 John 3:16). The love of his disciples, too, must be embodied—revealed in their bodies.

Day by day, Jesus offers us the totally embodied sign of his love with the words: "Take and eat; this is my body; this is the cup of my blood, drink from it."

TEMPLES OF GOD

The Christian's body, consecrated in baptism and sealed by the Spirit in confirmation, must be honored above all temples on earth; for it is, in a unique sense, a temple of God, a temple of the Holy Spirit. "Glorify God in your body" (1 Corinthians 6:20) becomes a theme song of Christian life. This temple of God, consecrated by God, must be kept holy.

In this same light, the Christian concept of chastity must be understood. The motive for chastity is absolutely positive: reverence for our bodies, for the physical and psychic dimensions of sexuality, reverence for the work of the Creator and Redeemer.

Our Christian prayer partakes of this embodiment. We raise our eyes and stretch our arms to heaven as a symbol of turning our hearts and minds to God. We meditate with all our senses, and the whole visible creation invites us to praise God.

The fundamental truth that the human body is a redeemed and consecrated temple presents us with another viewpoint. This is a temple which is, at all times and in all circumstances and activities, destined for the glory of God and the building up of the Mystical Body of Christ. The first requirement is that the whole person, in and through the body, radiates purity, reverence, peace, trust, fidelity.

> *Your eye is the lamp of your body. If your eye is healthy, your whole body is full of light; but if it is not healthy, your body is full of darkness. Therefore consider whether the light in you is not darkness. If then your whole body is full of light, with no part of it in darkness, it will be as full of light as when a lamp gives you light with its rays.*
>
> Luke 11:34-36

In light of Christ, men and women in their bodily realities are sacraments of a sort, effective signs of hope. The appearance of human beings, made in the image of God and able to cultivate and radiate spiritual values with their bodies, are the initial fulfillment of the divine promise and purpose of creation. This points to a still greater promise, the coming of the Word Incarnate, the Word of the Father made flesh. Having died on the cross, his glorified body is the supreme promise to the whole of creation and already an awesome fulfillment that opens up a new future. Jesus, crucified and risen, is the supreme, all-encompassing sacrament of hope for humanity and creation.

MEMBERS OF THE MYSTICAL BODY

Jesus continues to be a visible sign of hope also in his Mystical Body, the bodily life of his true disciples. They are called to embody this hope through their witness of faith, including their readiness to take upon themselves suffering whenever the victory of love, justice, and peace calls for it.

This witness to hope implies responsibility to the world, an ecological consciousness that perceptibly attests that Christ is the Savior of the whole world.

For the creation waits with eager longing for the revealing of the children of God; for the creation was subjected to futility, not of its own will but by the will of the one who subjected it, in hope that the creation itself will be set free from its bondage to decay and will obtain the freedom of the glory of the children of God. We know that the whole creation has been groaning in labor pains until now; and not only the creation, but we ourselves, who have the first fruits of the Spirit, groan inwardly while we wait for adoption, the redemption of our bodies.

Romans 8:19-23

It is surely God's will that we should discipline our bodies and keep them healthy. To abuse our bodies through unhealthy habits or lifestyles is to sin also against our psychic health, even against our salvation. By living healthily, we reach a harmonious wholeness that affords us greater energies, not only for work but also for better human relationships, and for the art of radiating peace and joy.

On the other hand, our bodies must never become idols. In our present-day culture, where many people no longer adore God, it is hardly surprising that idolatry of the body flourishes. What Paul warns against under other historical circumstances happens all too easily in our hedonistic consumer society. Many pamper their bodies to such an extent that they lose their spiritual strength. Their idolatrous cult of the body causes them to poison it with nicotine, alcohol, and dangerous drugs; they eat too much food while millions of people are dying of starvation.

Prayer

Lord, our God, how glorious is your name! "What are human beings that you are mindful of them, mortals that you care for them? Yet you have made them a little lower than God, and crowned them with glory and honor" (Psalm 8:4-5). The body of your incarnate Son has glorified you, and you have revealed in his risen body the fullness of glory and beauty. We thank you for the wonderful composition of our bodies, and for our calling to honor you in them. We praise you for having revealed that our bodies are meant to be temples, sealed and consecrated by the Holy Spirit.

Grant that we may understand this ever better in its implications for our lives. Pardon us for having paid so little attention to praising your name with respect to our bodies and those of our neighbors.

Lord Jesus, with your body you have given to God the greatest honor through its "dishonor" on the cross, its dishonor by sinners. Enlighten us with your Holy Spirit in times of sickness and suffering, and in the hour of our death, so that we may adore you in our bodies. Teach us to enjoy and admire the true beauty of our bodies which foreshadows the eternal glory in which they are to shine, and protect us from the danger of making sordid idols of them, your temples.

Love Chastely

So God created humankind in his image, in the image of God he created them; male and female he created them. God blessed them, and God said to them, "Be fruitful and multiply, and fill the earth and subdue it; and have dominion over the fish of the sea and over the birds of the air and over every living thing that moves upon the earth."...Then the LORD God formed man from the dust of the ground, and breathed into his nostrils the breath of life; and the man became a living being....Then the LORD God said, "It is not good that the man should be alone; I will make him a helper as his partner."...So the LORD God caused a deep sleep to fall upon the man, and he slept; then he took one of his ribs and closed up its place with flesh. And the rib that the LORD God had taken from the man he made into a woman and brought her to the man. Then the man said, "This at last is bone of my bones and flesh of my flesh; this one shall be called Woman, for out of Man this one was taken." Therefore a man leaves his father and his mother and clings to his wife, and they become one flesh.

Genesis 1:27-28; 2:7,18,21-24

In the Book of Genesis, God manifests a loving design for the world in the words which describe the origins of humankind. The Gospel of John enlightens us further about God's Word: "In the beginning was the Word....with God. All things came into being through him, and without him not one thing came into being" (John 1:1a,2b-3a).

The whole of creation has, somehow, the quality of a word, a revelation. But man and woman—because of their mutual rights and privileges—have a special mysterious relationship to God. Man and woman arrive at truth and self-knowledge when they discover the depths of language in their shared mutuality, in being with and for each other, knowing each other in love. Researchers think that the origins of human language is the language of love between man and woman, foreshadowed previously in the love songs of the birds and the love calls of other animals.

MARITAL CHASTITY

In biblical imagery, woman comes into being while the man is in a trance; and she too—like the man—yearns for mutuality and partnership. They are blessed by God, who creates them in the divine image for communion and companionship in mutual self-giving.

Man and woman should become, for each other, truthful "words," embodied and life-giving words, remindful of the divine covenant between them and a loving Creator. Each helps the other to become ever more visibly an image of God.

There is good biblical basis for today's theological endeavor to treat sexuality as embodied language which, in the marriage covenant and the faithfully fulfilled parental vocation, reaches the summit of communication in mutual self-giving. Men and women "reveal" themselves to each other in their relationships, and especially in the conjugal act if this is in total harmony with their daily "togetherness."

Sexuality is the way of being and relating to the world as a male or a female person. It embraces all the dimensions of physical, psychic, and spiritual manifestations experienced by each person. However, sexuality is to be understood neither as the principal identification of the human person, nor as a mere addition to it. Sexuality achieves its authentic totality only through integration with all our other dimensions and relationships. Its proper use will depend very much on how we recognize and honor the equal dignity and complimentarity of men and women as gifts of God.

CELIBATE LIFE

Even celibacy for the kingdom of God is greatly indebted to the multidimensional dialogue between mother and father and parents and children, without which young people would never have reached that level which allows them to love, with a Christ-like love, even those who otherwise are unloved. Consecrated celibacy by no means implies a kind of renunciation of manhood or womanhood. Although those who have freely chosen celibacy for the sake of the Lord renounce genital-sexual satisfaction, all their other means of communication—verbal and nonverbal—are marked by the complementarity and mutuality between men and women that is part of God's design for humankind.

Of itself, heterosexuality points toward marriage,

not by necessity but by free choice. According to God's plan, both marriage and celibacy are calls to service for the reign of God. Marriage is the ordinary way that this is done, while celibacy, by free choice, is the response to a special calling by God to answer the special needs of others. This does not mean, however, that it is extraordinary for young people to question whether or what should be their true vocation in life. On the contrary, it would be a sign of immaturity if a young Christian never posed this explicit question to himself or herself.

The free choice of celibacy for the reign of God can also be a helpful witness for those who remain or become single through no choice of their own, through death, divorce, etc. Such difficult situations can become fulfilled vocations and roads to holiness, even as it is for those who chose celibacy in the first place.

FAITHFUL LOVE

Both the way of marriage and the way of celibacy have their mystic joys and noble opportunities, but both also require a "yes" to the following of Christ crucified and a vigorous renunciation of all forms of selfishness. Only then can men and women develop their genuine capacities to love as sexual persons in their striving for love far beyond its sexual dimensions.

Sexuality, in the sense of bodily union, is fully and truly expressed only in marriage. Only there, consecrated to undying love and fidelity, do two partners truly become "one flesh." Sexual intercourse outside of marriage temporarily joins two bodies, but it does not make two persons "one flesh." However, in marriage, as in other states of life, the attainment of love and fidelity fluctuates in accord with the commitment of the spouses. For the redeemed, aiming toward perfection in truthfulness and faithfulness is indispensable, whether married or single, ordained or religious.

TRUTHFUL LOVE

Truthfulness is a decisive criterion in judging the authenticity of all expressions of love—whether by word, gesture, or bodily intimacy. Hence, in preparing for marriage and choosing a life partner, any words and gestures that awaken false hopes need to be avoided. The path that leads to the covenant of faithfulness should be marked by honesty and sincerity.

One of the most relevant consequences of this principle of absolute truthfulness is that sexual intercourse, in the sense of the profound mutual gift and the biblical "knowing" of each, is unthinkable outside the marriage covenant. Neither extramarital nor premarital intercourse is a truly conjugal experience. The commonplace sharing of beds, and even of homes, does not a covenant make. Nor do passionate vows of love and faithfulness, aimed at weakening the resolve to abstain from premarital sex.

The truthful expression of the mutual dependence of two persons who are created in the image of God, implies the recognition of the equal dignity of women and men. When equal dignity is fully acknowledged, the differences between us contribute to our mutual enrichment. We are at our best when we fully realize our high dignity and interdependence as image and likeness of God for each other.

Whenever another is desired as an object for the satisfaction of one's own lust, sexuality sinks beneath a shroud of lies and deceptions. Sex becomes cheap, trivial, a source of sadness and disgust. People who are slaves to senseless consumption in almost every area of life, have little chance to learn the chaste language of truthful love. But those who uphold their scale of values, while enjoying life and its gifts, are also better prepared to reap a rich harvest of joy in their sexual love and in their capacity to renounce whatever contradicts true love.

In an environment which abhors a rising birthrate, only a truly sincere conjugal and parental love can give convincing witness. Conjugal love is the only abiding source of generous, responsible parenthood.

What our world needs most are holy couples with the beauty and strength of conjugal and parental love, together with Christians who choose to live celibately and are disposed toward loving the unloved who are most in need of them.

Both marriage and celibacy severely challenge today's Christians, as we live in a superficial and deceitful environment. The manifest integrity of relationships between men and women are not possible without the grace of God, who is the source of all truth and love, and this must be acknowledged constantly in humble prayer and thanksgiving. Those who listen to the Word of God, cherish it in their hearts, and meditate on it together will best be able to accept one another as gifts of God, and to travel together on the path to ever more truthfulness, faithfulness, and love.

In all of life, aiming at mediocrity is doomed to failure. On the other hand, those who have solidified their fundamental option to pursue holiness need never be fainthearted. Even if they recognize that they have a long way to go to reach their ideal, they should not be discouraged. God sees their good will and blesses it.

Prayer

Gracious God, we extol your design in creating men and women to your image and likeness. We praise you for redeeming us in all our dimensions. Help us, whatever our state in life, to become ever more an image of your love, which is stronger than all the love of fathers and more tender than all the love of mothers.

Grant to your Church, and to our world, holy families. Guide and enlighten young people in discerning their states of life. Help them to find vocation, whether in marriage or in celibacy, for your reign. Strengthen and console those who, because of circumstances beyond their control, find themselves living celibate lives.

Assist all spouses in the face of crises, so that they can fully accept each other, pardon each other, bear the burden of each other, and grow in love. Fill us with your love and truth, so that we may live chastely in all our relationships, and grow together in the capacity to love the poorest among us: the unloved and alienated.

Respect Human Life

We do not live to ourselves, and we do not die to ourselves. If we live, we live to the Lord, and if we die, we die to the Lord; so then, whether we live or whether we die, we are the Lord's. For to this end Christ died and lived again, so that he might be Lord of both the dead and the living.

Romans 14:7-9

I came that they may have life, and have it abundantly. "I am the good shepherd. The good shepherd lays down his life for the sheep. The hired hand, who is not the shepherd and does not own the sheep, sees the wolf coming and leaves the sheep and runs away."

John 10:10b-12a

Divine life is the highest good, for which all other values are to be sacrificed; but to give our human life in the service of neighbors is the highest form of human love (see John 15:13). Thus, the tree of Christ's cross becomes the tree of life. Christ gives his life so that his friends might have fullness of life.

Essential to this fullness of life is a readiness to expose health and life to risks when serving others, and to do so in the discipleship of Christ. Since life is a precious good from God, this willingness deserves Jesus' praise. That is why he expresses thanks in the prayer of his life: "Sacrifices and offerings you have not desired, but a body you have prepared for me; in burnt offerings and sin offerings you have taken no pleasure. Then I said, 'See, God, I have come to do your will, O God'" (Hebrews 10:5-7).

There are too many people in the world who give legal status to the "art" of sacrificing the innocent lives of others in order to make their own lives more comfortable. Such people boast about freedom and the right of privacy. Mothers and doctors sacrifice millions of children in the womb, in order to diminish the guests at the table of life, or to prevent the "burden" of children who might be disabled in some manner.

The lives of all people are entrusted to our shared responsibility. By imitating the unselfish actions of the merciful Samaritan, we can rescue many who have fallen into the hands of "robbers."

SUPPORTING LIFE

If Christians would spend as much for the healing of lepers as they spend for harmful tobacco and alcohol, the plague of leprosy—which at the present time has about thirty million people in its grip—could be quickly overcome. I stand before each of my readers as a beggar for lepers. In many parts of the world, I have seen their sufferings.

Hundreds of millions of people suffer starvation, and millions of lives are threatened each year by hunger. These persons stretch out their arms to us for urgent help, indeed for generous help.

Our crusades against planned abortion, against wars and mass starvation, all must go hand in hand; otherwise we are inconsistent and not credible. Protests against the threat of nuclear weapons, which can destroy the whole of humankind, do well. But, while we protest, we need to ask ourselves if we are also willing to make our personal contributions to alleviate dangerous hunger and contagious diseases, or to take political action to bring about more generous help to the poorest countries. We should ask ourselves whether we are caring properly for our own health, or endangering the health of others.

Generous land developers and able medical missionaries are the merciful samaritans of today. During the course of a visit to a poor area of Africa, I met two Italian women—medical doctors—assisting there. Originally, they had volunteered for only a few years, but seeing the tremendous misery and need, they continued to prolong their stay. They have saved many lives. We could do something similar, simply by making generous offerings for the needs of others—offerings which, in many cases, can be lifesaving.

SAVING LIFE

Capital punishment is a "life" subject. There are opposing opinions on this, even within the Church. I oppose, on principle, the death penalty. I am convinced that this conviction is in keeping with the compassionate love of Christ and the heavenly Father for sinners. There are also historical reasons for this conviction. I allude especially to the German State under Hitler. Although modern judges are not to be accused of such crimes against life, they would do well to remember what happened in Hitler's time, and humbly to forbear passing the death penalty on people found guilty by fallible human judgment.

It cannot be denied that even in democratic countries "minorities" often receive the death penalty while the privileged class receives disproportionate or no punishment at all for the same kind of crimes. In general, we can assert that there exists such a shameful human tradition of judicial murder by communities all over the world.

We need, of course, to be tolerant of those who hold opposing views, but one thing needs to be vigorously asserted: A state which refuses to protect the innocent life of the unborn can claim no "legitimacy" for passing death penalties because the only "good" reason for a death penalty is the protection of "innocent" life against violence.

Prayer

*O God, Creator of all life, you seek not the death
of sinners but their conversion. We all live by your
generosity and mercy. We thank you for the
wonderful gift of being, to which you have added
the promise of eternal sharing in your life and
bliss. You have called all people to eternal life.
Help us, through your grace, to assist each other
on our road to fullness of being and eternal life.*

*We praise you, Father, for having sent us the Good
Shepherd, who has laid down his life and thus
has favored us with the sublime opportunity to
love our neighbors in the service of life, justice,
and peace. Make us witnesses to our faith and
hope in the resurrection of the body.*

*Merciful God, since earliest times people have
murdered their brothers and sisters, in time of
peace and even more in time of war, thus horribly
dishonoring your Name. We grieve, especially,
because even Christians neglect and even defy
your command to serve and save life, sinning
through both complicity and apathy. We all must
humbly ask ourselves if we have shown gratitude
for the gift of life through our wise and generous
shared responsibility for the life and health of our
brothers and sisters.*

*Forgive us, God, for having damaged our own
lives and those of others by an unreasonable,
unhealthy lifestyle. Make us signs of healing
goodness and peace, angels of nonviolent commitment to peace and justice.*

Heal Yourself
and Others

The disciples of John reported all these things to him. So John summoned two of his disciples and sent them to the Lord to ask, "Are you the one who is to come, or are we to wait for another?"...Jesus had just then cured many people of diseases, plagues, and evil spirits, and had given sight to many who were blind. And he answered them, "Go and tell John what you have seen and heard: the blind receive their sight, the lame walk, the lepers are cleansed, the deaf hear, the dead are raised, the poor have good news brought to them. And blessed is anyone who takes no offense at me."

Luke 7:18-19,21-23

Holy Scripture leaves no doubt that healing the sick is an essential dimension of Christ's mission. On some occasions it seems that, for him, healing is more urgent than preaching the Good News; or rather, healing the sick is a privileged form of proclaiming the Good News. He heals even on the Sabbath, although he knows that this makes him a stumbling block for the legalists.

The sermon on the plain is introduced thus: "And all in the crowd were trying to touch him, for power came out from him and healed all of them" (Luke 6:19). Healing is a manifestation, not only of his power but, above all, of his compassionate love. Jesus seems to see in disease an aspect of the powers of evil, a sign of a world in need of redemption and liberation. Healing the sick is also a symbol of the healing of those with broken hearts. Yet, Jesus vigorously rejects the prevailing opinion of his time: that the sick and/or their parents are cursed because of their sins (see John 9:2-3). Especially lepers suffered severely from this notion. They were outcasts, untouchable, and despised as the most miserable of sinners. Jesus reaches out to them, heals them, and reintegrates them into society, thus restoring them to religious and civic esteem.

By his healing activities, Jesus glorifies his Father. He also points out that patient suffering is one way of following him on the way of the cross. Nevertheless, acceptance of suffering and illness in ourselves and others has a positive meaning only if we do everything possible to heal whatever can be healed.

Modern medicine has won many battles against disease, and will win many more. At the same time, however, our contemporary world, with its unhealthy lifestyles and its reckless abuse and destruction of the environment, has opened the door for legions of evils. This warns us that we should not simply resign ourselves to sickness as if it were "sent" by God. We should not blame God for the many evils we have brought upon ourselves.

Nevertheless, while doing our best to heal what can be healed and removing the causes of sickness where they can be removed, we can resolutely accept the burden of shared responsibility for what cannot be healed—even as Jesus took upon his shoulders the cross which human iniquity had prepared for him. We may detest all sins, including those which have disrupted our world and caused diseases, while still bearing our own crosses in times of illness. We would not be true disciples of Christ if we cursed our sufferings. Our just rebellion against the sinful causes of evil must never become rebellion against God who, in times of sickness, gives us strength to endure every ordeal.

HEALTH OF BODY AND SOUL

Before we consider the important question of what health has to do with salvation and holiness, we should clarify what we mean by human health. Health does not consist of the mere bodily capability of working, although this is an excellent quality to have. Nor is it sheer bodily strength, especially when the higher faculties that reach out for truth and search for ultimate meaning are neglected. Human health can be defined as the highest possible embodiment of the spirit and the noblest spiritualization of the bodily dimension. One person's body may have a surplus of physical vitality, but a pitiful lack of openness to the spirit and to healthy human relations. Another person's body, although physically suffering, may be completely open to the spirit of goodness, joy, peace, compassion, and serenity. A well-trained body makes for an excellent person if it is guided by its higher values.

The physical integrity of the body and all its vital parts is a precious good entrusted to our personal and shared responsibility. But this kind of integrity falls short of human wholeness and health. On the one hand, there are ways of risking health which do violence to wholeness and our vocation to wholeness. On the other hand, there can be generous commitments involving substantial risk to physical health which are genuine expressions of the pursuit of holiness in the service of neighbor and the common good.

Of great relevance to wholeness, salvation, and promotion of salvation is psychic health, but even here we have to be cautious in our evaluation. Recently, I was informed of the death of a dear friend, a genial man in many respects. After undergoing the shocking experiences of Hitler's war, his proneness to depression caused a nervous breakdown. He began to speak out publicly against the war crimes of Hitler, and only the intervention of a psychiatrist saved him from being executed. Later, we often talked about his situation, which he shrewdly analyzed. Thanks to modern medicine, his condition was kept under control, but what helped him more than the drugs was his astonishingly serene conformity with God's will. Beyond and above the psychic illness, there was a feeling and force of wholeness which allowed him to accept and transcend his disability.

Psychosomatic medicine, psychoanalysis, and the

various schools of psychotherapy have revolutionized the concepts of health, sickness, and healing. Attention centers largely on the phenomenon of neuroses. In a neurotic state, essential energies are blocked by unfavorable conditions in the environment, by disturbed human relationships, and by unresolved personal problems. These forces, even though they are not properly brought to the fore or cultivated, are not dead. When they do not find a healthy outlet, they turn inward, causing extreme tensions and singular reactions. It would be a great error, and an injustice, to malign persons suffering neuroses or to impose moral condemnations on them. A neurosis should be understood as a cry from the depths for inner wholeness and healthy relationships, a cry for someone who can help to uncover these inner forces and their meaningful use.

HEALTH AND WHOLENESS

Victor Frankl, the father of logotherapy, has drawn our attention to neogenic neurosis, which develops in an existential vacuum when the inborn desire for ultimate meaning is frustrated. The conscious and frequently unconscious loss of meaning, or repression of the search for meaning, disturbs both somatic and psychic health. The lack of harmony between achievement or pleasure-seeking and failure to establish a scale of values, affects people in all their dimensions and relationships. Healing requires a new impetus in the search for meaning, and the gradual realization of the level of meaning provided by insight. Here we see the fixed relation between health and wholeness/holiness.

The experiences of logotherapists suggests that

those who graciously and patiently help other persons
in their search for meaning provide the kind of therapy
that is so necessary in seeking redemption. Persons
who are physically or psychically sick, or disabled, are
most seriously threatened in their wholeness and salvation if they fail to search for the meaning of life, or
refuse to find an acceptable meaning for their suffering. To feel secure in the attainment of a value which
fills the heart and mind is a giant step on the road to
human health.

In the tedious struggle against sin, and the constant
striving for holiness, an especially profound experience
of God's purifying fire can deeply affect persons in
need of thoroughgoing purification. It is equally true,
however, that a sincere friendship with Christ, and the
experience of God's nearness and love, create aston-
ishing energies for building wholeness and human
health in all its dimensions. The inner peace and last-
ing serenity which are God's gifts to those who seek
only to conform with his will, provide amazing strength
to cope with life's tasks and tests. This inner harmony,
reflecting union with God, is also a blessing for bodily
and psychic health.

Viktor von Weizsäcker, a prominent physician, says,
"illness is a mode of being human." We have to pass
through the experience of weakness, unhealthiness,
and finally death, on our way to eternal life. If—in the
various situations of life—we accept God's design to
the best of our ability, then even grave suffering and
illness can become times of grace. Illness reminds us
of the finiteness and frailty of earthly life; it challenges
us not to lose sight of heavenly life with God. Thus it is
an offer and an opportunity for deeper reflection and

clearer direction toward our abiding vocation. We have to see both risk and opportunity in illness. In the school of the crucified, illness presents us with a favorable time to become better friends of Christ.

Prayer

Protect us, O Lord, from all sinful neglect of our health. Heal us, for we have sinned against you and against our own wholeness. Grant that a healthy soul may dwell in our body and radiate purity and peace, whether our body be weak or strong.

Grant us deeper insight into the meaning of life, health, and unhealthiness. But, above all, bestow on us that love which guarantees that every-thing—suffering and ill-health included—will redound for our good.

Give us the grace and the strength to care more for salvation and holiness than for mere physical health, and yet to care enough for health not to lessen our striving for holiness and unselfish service.

Gracious God, assist and console the sick. Enlighten and heal those who have failed to search diligently for the true meaning of life and, as a consequence, are sick in body and soul. Send loving and competent people into their lives, to guide them in renewed yearning for a meaningful life.

Meditate on Your Mortality

But in fact Christ has been raised from the dead....so all will be made alive in Christ. But each in his own order: Christ the first fruits, then at his coming those who belong to Christ.

Then comes the end, when he hands over the kingdom to God the Father, after he has destroyed every ruler and every authority and power. For he must reign until he has put all his enemies under his feet. The last enemy to be destroyed is death....When this perishable body puts on imperishability, and this mortal body puts on immortality, then the saying that is written will be fulfilled: "Death has been swallowed up in victory." "Where, O death, is your victory? Where, O death, is your sting?" The sting of death is sin, and the power of sin is the law. But thanks be to God, who gives us the victory through our Lord Jesus Christ.

1 Corinthians 15:20a,22b-26,54-57

Death is surely our abiding companion. Our lives are passageways to death, whether we like it or not. Christians who consciously live by faith are familiar with death. They know its awesomeness; but they rely on God's firm promise that, with the help of divine grace, a faithful confirmation of their vocation to holiness will make the day of their death a harvest feast, a victory celebration of their fidelity to Christ, a coming home to the Father.

Those who banish the thought of death are doomed to an unreal mode of existence. With no convictions about life's final truth, they are swayed by the masses who do not want to know where they are going. Those who plan their lives as if death did not await them are more "under the law of death" than they suspect. A stubborn determination not to face death and not to accept it as part of a person's truth blocks all access to life's truth.

Those who affirm life's and death's final meaning as consciously and trustingly as Paul did, will experience the same liberation from slavish fear of death and law. One dying man expressed this beautifully when his doctor was nervously searching for words to tell him that death was near: "Doctor, are you having trouble telling me that I am going to die? Why? All my life I have lived for this day!"

Solidarity in Christ, complete union with him through his redemption, leads to the joyous song of praise: "Thanks be to God, who gives us the victory through our Lord Jesus Christ" (1 Corinthians 15:57).

OUR ATTITUDE

A right attitude toward illness and death is a basic question of social ethics. The world needs our effort, our witness, and our wisdom for the liberating truth. It is a matter of shared courage to accept all of life's dimensions in the fullness of their truth. The profile of society itself is transformed when we frankly acknowledge that we all walk together in the shadow of death.

This freedom to accept each day of our lives as an approach to death is anchored in our faith in the Resurrection of Christ and in the divine promise of our own resurrection.

Death is natural. Our whole biological frame is directed toward growth and gradual decrease, leading naturally to death. However, *our* dying is something totally different from the dying of plants and animals. Our death is a decision to be consciously faced.

Yet, there is also something very unnatural about human death—especially the death of sinners. The flood of sin, growing from its poisoned beginnings into a stream of anguish and terror, is not willed by God. Sinners, closing their hearts to redemption, making their choices against salvation-solidarity and thereby locking themselves into the guilt of sin-solidarity, cannot blame God or nature for the anguish and futility surrounding their deaths.

Given the unnaturalness of unredeemed sinfulness, it is "natural" for sinners to banish the thought of death, to rebel against it, and to suffer the terrible consequences of this flight and rebellion. But the redeemed, who by God's grace build their lives on faith in redemption and resurrection, are indeed liberated from the "law of death" that sinners choose. At death—by the power of grace and faith—a real transformation takes place: the believing redeemed who die with Christ take on an abiding "life in Christ."

In accord with God's design, we are all meant to be liberated from the terrible death which befits the sinner as sinner—a death which is a sign of solidarity in sin and futility. Christ, accepting the anguish of the most painful and humiliating death on the cross, echoes the anguished cry of sinful humanity: "My God, my God, why have you forsaken me?" He offers himself as redemptive sacrifice in the supreme act of saving-solidarity. He, who by divine mission is saving-justice and saving-solidarity, he who is without sin, consents to the Passover through the Red Sea of sin-solidarity and its bitter consequences.

We, who put our faith in Christ's saving death and Resurrection, are liberated from death as punishment and final despair. Yet death still possesses painful dimensions, even for true believers. The first is that most of us are not yet fully detached from all sin; we are not living fully in Christ. Physical pain and mental anguish brought on by separation from loved ones—which, in accord with God's design, is a sharing of saving-solidarity with our Redeemer—give us abundant opportunities to overcome, with God's grace, this laxness in our faith. But a more important and consoling fact is that, for those called to share Christ's redeeming action in the world, it is—in a way—"natural" to consciously accept the pains of illness and death "for the life of the world." It becomes a passover of solidarity, from the inglorious death of the unredeemed to the glorious death of the redeemed. It is the seed that falls to the ground to become new and wonderful life.

We firmly believe this important truth: Death is in no way a curse or a punishment. Even the painful fact of knowing that we need further purification is pervaded by the consoling light of the paschal mystery. The final transformation at death is most apparent in those who accept death, with all its external circumstances, as a gracious presence of the Giver of eternal life, who brings to completion everything God has begun and favored throughout our lifetime.

One of the most precious faith experiences we can have is to be present at the bedside of a dying Christian who gives convincing testimony that "dying is gain and living is Christ." We should never stop praying for the undeserved grace of perseverance in God's love for ourselves and those we love, indeed for all believers. It is also a matter of fundamental saving-solidarity that we help the dying to receive the consolation of the sacraments as frequently as possible, and to receive all the pastoral care they need.

OUR RESPONSIBILITY

As active Christians, we shall do our best to ensure that no one within our sphere of influence will die the fearful death of the unredeemed, a death encountered in guilt and alienation, a death endured after desertion or open rebellion.

Under the heading of "unnatural," we consider, first and foremost, deaths due to suicide or murder. We have to ask ourselves how many other people have participated, actively or passively, in the process of decay that leads to such outbreaks of unnaturalness.

Penal law speaks of "manslaughter" when punishable negligence contributes to the unnatural death of others. Negligence can take a thousand forms. Reckless driving is one of the most frequent, but the fault may also lie with irresponsible people who take "just one more" drink before driving, with careless drivers who neglect the maintenance and repair of their cars, with those who drive when they are depressed or angry or exhausted, and with countless others who are guilty of culpable negligence on the road.

Millions of people burn out life's energies and shorten their life spans by an immoderate use of alcohol, drugs, and tobacco. Their sometimes early deaths— "unnatural," in our sense of the word—point to the frightening evil of collective sin: neglect by parents, educators, pastors, moral theologians, and by doctors who do not want to be accused of "moralism"—while, indeed, their own neglect in this matter is immoral.

It is also immoral to judge those who, for various reasons, die early or violently. Redemption does not allow us simply to point to culprits. Rather, we should look after our own responsibility and continue to examine our own consciences.

EUTHANASIA

Etymologically, *euthanasia* means "dying well." Understood in a Christian sense, this includes: a striving for a good life, which is the best preparation for a good death; a heartfelt assent to life and death; a loving care for the dying, given by families, friends, and neighbors, and especially by the members of the healing professions; an attempt to alleviate the sufferings of terminal illness; and a reassuring effort to emphasize the consolation of faith.

In today's medical-ethical discussions, euthanasia means both the refusal of helpful measures in order to speed the arrival of death, and the use of measures intended to cause death directly.

Theologians, backed by the teaching authority of the Church, categorically condemn both of the above methods. Euthanasia is an attack on God's sovereignty over death and life. Consciously to cause one's own death, or to ask others to cooperate in it, or to refuse helpful means to which the dying or gravely ill person has a right, are all arbitrary acts deserving of condemnation. If death-promoting methods are used without the consent of the sick person, and with the explicit intention to cause death, this is, of course, simply murder.

Euthanasia, whether in the sense of refusal of helpful treatment with the purpose of shortening life, or in the sense of direct measures to accelerate death, is not only a moral problem, but also a legislative one. We do not command the state to place penal sanctions on all transgressions of ethical principles; but to legalize euthanasia, or to legally declare that the state leaves such decisions to private individuals, is a betrayal of the state's specific duty. Its duty is to protect the weak, the aged, the sick, and the disabled: to protect the sacredness of human life.

Quite different is the use of intense painkillers, or the courageous attempt to save life by unusual means when ordinary means have failed, even at the risk of shortening life unintentionally. These do not conform to the concept of euthanasia which we radically reject.

RIGHT TO BE INFORMED

Another matter that concerns each of us personally, and is highly relevant for Christians who participate in the formation of public opinion, is the right of patients—especially the terminally ill—to be truthfully informed about their situation. Truthfulness is essential for healthy personal relationships and for healthy communities. It has special relevance in the patient/doctor relationship.

Of course, an unfavorable diagnosis is not a truth that can always be communicated bluntly and instantly to the sick person. Failure to give all the facts at once is not a lie if the intention is to tell the truth, step-by-step, in the best possible manner. Doctors, nurses, and members of the family can tactfully probe, to determine to what extent the patient is ready to hear the full truth, or to receive further information. It is best for patients to help the doctor out, by showing their readiness and courage to face the truth. When my larynx cancer recurred, I told the doctor emphatically that I support the principle that "only truth can liberate us." I could see that the doctor immediately felt at ease, and he did not hesitate to explain the facts to me.

In recent years, almost every country has discussed the advisability of human transplants: the transfer of healthy organs—from a person who has just died—to ailing people in need of them. Legislators who weigh this situation have to choose between two possibilities: either to allow doctors to make lifesaving use of

organs of the deceased as soon as death is certain
(unless there is explicit protest by a last will or by
family members), or to invite people—by way of their
final wills—to donate their organs for use after their
death. The second possibility seems the more ideal, if
indeed a sufficient number of people thus generously
extend—beyond their death—their responsibility for
the life and health of others by donating the use of
their organs. But I also see no serious objection to the
first possibility, when this concurs with public opinion and actually helps to save more lives.

Prayer

*We praise you and thank you, Lord Jesus Christ,
for having conquered sin-solidarity through your
death and Resurrection, and for having inducted
all who believe in you into saving-solidarity,
which gives new meaning to the death of believers.
We thank you for having done everything to free
us from the law of anguish-filled death.*

*Each time we participate in the Eucharist, we
praise and proclaim your death and Resurrection
until you come to conduct us into the eternal
reign of God.*

*We pray for the grace to persevere in your love,
and we ask for a good death for ourselves and for
all people, so that we finally can confide our lives
into your hands.*

*Holy Mary, Mother of God, pray for us sinners,
now and at the hour of our death.*